Life Under Construction

...a work in progress

Dr. Maryellen Lipinski

Life Under Construction...*a work in progress*

by Dr. Maryellen Lipinski

Copyright © 2003

All rights reserved. No part of this book may be reproduced in any form or by any electronic or mechanical means, including information storage and retrieval systems, without permission in writing from the author, except by a reviewer who may quote brief passages in a review.

Lipinski, Maryellen, 1951-

ISBN Number 0-9742743-1-3

Maryellen Lipinski, Ed.D.
www.maryellenlipinski.com
All rights reserved

First Edition
Printed in the United States of America
LUC Press
November 2003

The quotations in the book were gathered with love and yet very unscientifically over many years. To the authors and original sources – Thank You! My apologies if they do not appear exactly as they were once voiced.

Talent is helpful in writing

but guts are absolutely necessary.

🐚 Jessamyn West

There is no agony like

bearing an untold story

inside you.

🌱 Zora Neale Hurston

Books are like imprisoned souls till someone takes them down from a shelf and frees them.

≈ Sammuel Butler

Thanks,
    Maryellen

ACKNOWLEDGEMENTS WITH LOVE

Dad - survived another one of my moves, even though he did not understand.

Paul & Vanessa - for their support during my move and continued love, even though they did not want me to go. Special thanks to Paul, who helped me with the heavy boxes!

Michele Fedderly - my best friend for over 25 years whose integrity is unparalleled.

Sam Horn - a talented author with never ending optimism and encouragement for my work.

Jodi Walker & Barb Geraghty - My first mountain visitors who made "ooh" and "ah" sounds upon their visit.

Steve Gajda - my constant source of information when building my home.

Judy and Jan at Fairfield - guided me through the architectural review committee meeting as helped me avoid fines during the building process.

Tommy & the crew at HJennings Hardware and Building Supply Store. They save me several times from making BIG mistakes.

Billy - my mountain man and good friend. He took some of the photos.

Colene - for getting me to these mountains.

Richard Morrison, A.I.A. - a friend who gave me very professional and generous architectural advice.

jc - 1st friend to visit my lot. He said, "You're not just moving across the country, you are moving into another land." He was excited anyway.

Finally - to my three volunteer proofreaders, Patricia, Paul & Pat!

Table of Contents

BEGINNING of a New Chapter in My Life 1

Life Under Construction...a work in progress 3

Cashiers, North Carolina 6

A New Life in an Old Land 11

Buying a Lot 17

Happy Birthday 26

Are You at Home in Your Life? 30

Plans 34

Firing my GC 38

Confiscated Plans 45

Life By Design	48
Building a Home-A Different Animal	58
The First Peg	63
Renovate Your Mind	68
Reconstructing Your Time	74
Restoring Your Energy	80
Lessons Learned	85
Signals and Signs in the Universe	86
Celebrations of Country Living	88
Mountain Moon	90
Handling Imperfections	95

I've Got An Itch 97

Mental Preparation................................ 99

The One Unknown................................ 104

Moonshine to Champagne 105

Moving In.. 108

Write Your Own Building Permit 111

END... 114

Mel's Mountain Dream Home

BEGINNING OF A NEW CHAPTER IN MY LIFE

In the end of my book Random Thoughts and Mine Always Are: Conscious Detours to Creative Power, I wrote about my decision to move from California to North Carolina to live in the mountains of Western North Carolina, a bit more country to say the least.

I looked at this as making a new life in an old land. Many of my friends and at times even I, entertained the thought and did not hesitate to ask why I was moving again. I certainly thought it was a fair question. I wondered if I would ever settle somewhere. Would I ever be satisfied to stay in one place? Then I looked at my decision in a different light. Why not always be searching? Why not keep a dream ahead of you guiding the way? Anytime you let go of something limiting, you create space for something better.

As I sit in my magical mountain home writing this, I am gazing out the window at the powdery blush of mountain laurel in full bloom. The beauty of the sun kissing each limb of the tree as it lowers its head for the night, strikes me. I watch in awe as it disappears over the mountain ridge.

Life Under Construction...*a work in progress*

I have come to believe that one never knows where life is going or how long it will last.

A few words about the title of this book. Life is forever under construction and the reality of life is that it is always a work in progress. It's ongoing, always changing and fluid. Even the best-laid plans need reconstructing, restoring, reframing, and renovating at times.

Two great words: work and progress. Progress is work most of the time, although I must admit, I have made progress at times by doing nothing except waiting. I'm not too good at patience. What happens it seems is that instead of calmness, fear seeps in. What I have learned to do, however, is remember that trusting the universe does work. And it works in the universe's order, not mine. So, forward movement can mean no movement at all. But we are moving, moving towards a destination and developing towards a better, more complete condition, even if we have doubts about our progress.

An excitement about life changes can accompany life's progress. And oh, the feeling of apprehension and vulnerability permeates the air. Why does it seem that confidence wavers so often? Am I the only one who feels it? Does it happen to you?

When it happens, I stop to remember. Life is always changing and evolving. Life is never really complete. Even knowing this, it is still hard to accept. We are never really finished as the progress of living goes on and on.

This book puts emphasis and special importance on life as a work in progress, asking the following questions:

Are you the architect of your future?

Are you building the life you really want to live?

Are you using quality materials?

And finally, are you at home in your life?

> *Three things to be looked at in a building,*
> *that it stands on the right spot,*
> *that it be securely founded,*
> *and that it be successfully executed.*
>
> ~ Goethe

The above quote describes my journey to becoming the architect of my home and it seems to work when thinking about the future as well.

Let's start building!

Cashiers, North Carolina

It's a bit ironic that the main intersection in Cashiers is called "The Crossroads." Well, actually it's the only intersection with the only traffic light in town. I arrived in Cashiers on March 28, 2000, at a time when I felt I was at a crossroads in my life — a point at which a vital decision must be made.

I moved here in search of a different pace of life. I wanted to sit by a rushing creek and meander around a lake surrounded by mountains. Where the flowers would shout out for me to come take a peek. Where I could get in my car and take a short drive to find a waterfall, grand mountain views, simple weathered barns, tiny towns and roads less traveled. The nature of Cashiers is beautiful and everything I had hoped it would be, and this is even after having survived my first "winter."

The crossroads is marked where US Highway 64 and NC Highway 107 meet and it falls between two points of the Eastern

Continental Divide. Population during the winter months, rounded off, is 1,700 residents. It's quite a bit busier in the summer months when people seek relief from the hot summer sun and spend time in the mountains, where the summer breezes are cool and the air is fresh and the living is easy.

I had found refuge in Cashiers for twenty years when I needed a break from my hectic life and was in search of fall color. In California, where I lived near the beach, I did not experience a change of seasons. I realized as much as I loved the weather, it became too predictable for me. It was time for a change of seasons. Living here now, I am not disappointed by the beauty, silence and unpredictability of the mountains.

Let me set the stage and describe where I have moved with a bit more detail. Cashiers is described as "an outdoor holiday" in one chamber of commerce brochure. It's a quiet corner of southwestern North Carolina, a green valley 3,500 feet high surrounded by mountains rising up to 5,000 feet.

The mountains surrounding Sapphire Valley, where my home is, and about five miles outside of town, are said to be older than the Alps, Andes or the Rockies. Thirteen hundred species of flowering plants and 131 species of trees and over 300 varieties of minerals make their home here. I'm hoping I just might find a sapphire in my stream. It's a mighty special place with a history of its own. Hernando DeSoto passed through in 1540.

Spring brings abundant mountain laurel, rhododendron and azaleas. Summer is lush and green. Autumn is ablaze with color and winter glistens with falling snow on occasion. There are some 20,000 acres of national forest and more than 2,000 liquid acres of lakes in this scenic valley.

Maybe after experiencing my book, you might just want to explore Cashiers for yourself. By all means, drop by my neighborhood and come visit. It's small enough that you'll be sure to find me. I'll probably be in the Schoolhouse. That's the name of our local coffee house where I can order a cup of coffee named after my nickname, Mel. I'll be in the corner, writing away and savoring each sip of java, keeping my promise to myself to slow down. It's okay to interrupt me. I'll appreciate the break.

*If what I say resonates with you,
it is merely because we are branches
on the same tree.*

🌿 W. B. Yeats

Schoolhouse - Coffee Shop in Cashiers, NC.

A New Life in An Old Land

I tend to remember birthdays, especially my own. In fact, I have been known to celebrate my birthday for the entire month of May. I love my own, so I celebrate my friends' as well. My friends are special and these are their days. After not calling a friend on her birthday, something I had done for over 20 years, she knew something was wrong. Sure enough, she was right.

It was about day five in bed and the phone rang. I knew enough to pick it up. I took a deep breath and felt some relief. A human contact in the world was most welcomed.

Relief and tears welled up in my eyes as I pushed out the one simple word, hello. As old friends can intuitively sense another friend's inner movements, she said, "I'm on my way. I'll be there tomorrow." Tomorrow arrived and the doorbell rang. It was a long, slow and shaky journey down the 12 steps to the front door. It was the first time I had been up and about for days. Colene took one look at me and told me to lie down on the couch. She came over and, with her soothing voice, said nothing of what I expected her to say, essentially about how I was feeling. Instead, she uttered the words, "You need to move to North Carolina. All your furniture in your house looks like mountain furniture anyway."

The light may have gone on for Colene, but all I saw was darkness and fear. My focus was on living and getting healthy, not moving. When she left the next day, she said, "See you in North Carolina." She was preparing to move there in a month or so.

I was feeling triumphant just because I made it downstairs and she was talking about a move across the country. Less than one year later, I was taping my first box for my journey to the mountains.

When you make a big move, it impacts you both physically and emotionally. It's important to "let go" of ties to the old way of doing things. Let go of being too attached to the outcomes and focus on making the right choices for your new life. I'm not sure there is an easy method for approaching it but I think of Eleanor Roosevelt's quote: "Face the fear and do it anyway."

Most of my transitions in life have been after major events. I constantly strive for balance but the truth is, I can run hot and cold. You know, I think some people just quietly grow in insight and then others need a good splash of ice water to initiate a change. I, apparently fit within the latter category. My first major life move was from Florida to California following a foot injury that provided me with some time to think and forced me to slow down. I was the director of a drug and alcohol treatment center and working about 90 hours a week. I lasted three years. I also had a private practice in psychology which was tense, to say the least. Basically, I never slept through the entire night without a phone call. The time on crutches helped me finally "get it." Meaning, I had no life. So, I moved 3,000 miles from Sarasota, Florida, to San Francisco, California, to start a new life and career. When I make a move, it's usually a "big" one.

The second major move, from Newport Beach, California, to the mountains of Western North Carolina, took place after a bout of pneumonia and pericardial infusion (fluid around the heart). In 2000, I lost a dear friend to leukemia. I would not be brave enough to pray for trauma but somehow it works out well for me. I was exhausted. I recovered enough to finally get a doctor's clearance to travel to Italy. After planning and looking forward to this trip for over two years, I stayed three weeks. It was not long enough. At any rate, I came alive again. The message to construct a different life for myself was vivid. If Italy cannot bring you alive, nothing can. I think I am Polish Italian.

And then the thought entered my feeble mind. At this stage it was a fleeting thought. Why not give yourself a fabulous fiftieth birthday present? Why not build a dream home in the mountains. I nestled in as I imagined the slower life that awaited me, but my mind chuckled and said, "yeah-right!"

There is something about moving and starting fresh, especially in a land of ancient mountains. Some say, once the highest in the world. It is as if you can hear the earth talking to you. For me, there is comfort in being surrounded by the wisdom that the mountains hold.

Each time I imagine that a move might get easier, it usually doesn't, but it can get more exciting. It certainly gives us a hint of how secure one is in our inner world. The world where walls can be inches thick, with layer upon layer of growth. Maybe even a touch moldy and a bit slimy surrounded by lots of dust and dirt. As you peel off the layers, you reveal your true self. I am hopeful you can learn some truths about your own life that will somehow enrich and deepen your appreciation for constructing your future.

Yep, I knew it was time to make yet another move, another change. I needed to slow down once again.

The notes I handle no better than many pianists. But the pauses between the notes— ah, that is where the art resides.

ಈ Arthur Schnabel

Buying A Lot

I was casually heading toward my fiftieth year and wondered what I would give myself for my birthday. I considered this one of the BIG ones. Which means that I deserve something really special. Then it hit me again. Why not a home in the mountains? Sure, why not. I'm only 50 once.

It was harder than it sounded. Since I could not find the "perfect" mountain home, I decided to build, but first, I had to find the ideal lot.

"You can't have a view and a stream." "Why not?" I asked. "Because it just doesn't work that way," said my real estate agent. "Why is that?" I asked. "In your price range, it just doesn't." It doesn't? "Sure it does!" I said. I just had to find it.

And so my search began. I looked at over 50 lots. Well, that is all I will admit to. The actual number is lost somewhere in my brain. I think it is called denial. I hiked half of them, and I mean hiked. These lots are dense and require walking into masses of brush, laurel and trees with no path of any degree. You just push through and use your imagination. Why is imagination important? Because you have to envision a view from 16-20 feet higher than you are standing. Imagine the winter and summer views. This part was a bit easier on my third trip because it was in November and the fallen leaves allowed a peek into the space behind them. And then I found it!

I finally found my dream lot in the mountains. I hiked all the way to the property lines. The lot was about one acre. I heard a wonderful sound in the distance. A stream. A stream was gently rolling with delight along the smooth faces of each rock. At last, I was ready to build. Relief and exhaustion set in. I had it. A view and a stream. Time to buy.

I was feeling overwhelmed and full of joy as I drove to my

realtor's office, ready to make an offer. I made it and signed the papers and started to review my house plans. And then it happened. The words of disappointment rang through my ears like a freight train. My realtor said the lot had a pending sale on it. Someone had already made an offer and my realtor did not know this. I felt the color drain from my face. My spirit took a deep dive and the rain poured both inside and outside.

Did I have the energy to start all over again?

I traveled back to California for three weeks and then headed back to North Carolina to start the hunt once more. After days of searching, I saw Lot 66 on the market. I could tell by the plat that it backed up to Lot 40, the lot I did not get. I pulled the ladder out of the jeep and dragged it out to the middle of the property. Understand, just to get to the middle involved trudging through sticker bushes, fallen trees and the possibility of stepping on snakes. I climbed to the top of the ladder and imagined sitting on the top of my deck. There was definitely a winter view. I could tell this because of the fallen leaves. Just a short walk to my stream revealed a very modest waterfall. A bonanza! I knew there was a stream on the property, even though the owners did not. This was the lot. This time my friend was with me. Even Thumper, my friend's dog, was jumping around happily and running through the trees with vim, vigor and oomph in celebration.

In the back of our minds, we both remembered having seen some other buyers following along looking at the same lots, using a hack saw to plunge into the forest. My heart started beating rapidly and my friend got rather hysterical. She advised me that I'd better make up my mind fast or I might lose this one. She said, "I bet they want to buy it." Panic began to fill my veins and race to my heart. I had that "throw up" feeling in my stomach. I could not go through losing another lot. Like a fire engine racing to a fire, we flew down the mountain to the real estate office to try once again. I whispered to my friend, "This is happening so fast. I'm not sure." At this time I not only meant about lots but also what I was doing with my life. Did I miss anything? Once again, I'd found it. Or did I?

A view and a stream. With relief and anticipation, I made an offer. They accepted, and now you are hearing the rest of the story. Lot 66 was mine. I owned about an acre of property in the Western North Carolina Mountains.

The next time I flew to North Carolina and drove up to visit my lot, there was a bright red wooden sign nailed to a tree that proudly read, "Maryellen's." I hung some wind chimes on a tree, smiled and left once again for California.

P.S. While I am writing this, Lot 40, the first lot, has come back on the market. A coincidence? I think not. For some reason, I was meant to be in this space.

It is the nature of any organic building

to grow from its site,

come out of the ground into light.

           🌿 Frank L. Wright

*Things
do not change;
We
change.*

🍂 Henry David Thoreau

Not Just an Empty Lot, but the Beginning of My Dream.

Only the heart knows how to find what is precious.

🍂 Fyodor Dostoevsky

The Stream Behind my Home.

The Spirit of the Mountains.

Happy Birthday!

My first book ended with me struggling to find the words that would allow me to describe to my California friends why I was leaving and heading toward the Western North Carolina Mountains. My response at the time was, "It just suits me." My response now is, "This is where I have belonged all my life." I am home. I knew it the minute my plane landed in Asheville, North Carolina. For good, this time.

For years I was looking forward to celebrating my fiftieth birthday with precious friends. They were planning a delightful get together to celebrate my life. I'm not much for official planned parties but this was a day that I was looking forward to this one time event. And then it happened. I moved. I wasn't even close to my dear friends when my birthday actually arrived. I was in North Carolinas surrounded by the beauty of the mountains.
As per my usual style, I took the long way around when I moved to North Carolina from California by way of New Zealand. My house in California sold in four days so it was time to move

ready or not. I had work in New Zealand and decided after finishing there, I would just fly directly to the house that I rented in North Carolina.

After about a 48-hour journey, I arrived in Asheville. It was dark and interestingly eerie. The looming mountains took on a mysterious persona. The drive from the airport was only about 44 miles but remember I was heading into the mountains and the last 10 miles were "country miles". Basically, that means it takes you twice as long to cover the same distance on most any other road. I arrived surrounded by fog and not yet accustomed to the endless-curvy mountain roads. I was eager to stop turning 90 degrees. I tried to drag from my mind the history of the next curve, but it was useless because I couldn't even see the next bend. But none of that really mattered because I was now going to be living in the mountains. I took a long deep breath.

Life takes it own course. My desire to move to the mountains and slow down had a strong drive with a pull of its own. I made it! I was living in the mountains on my fiftieth birthday.

And then there was another birthday present. Well, you only turn 50 once. I finally "let go" of a car to which I was very attached for way too long and bought a brand new "jeep." Well, I was living in the mountains now. My old car had become a symbol to me. A sign of longevity and my determination to take care of something over time. I bought this Mercedes; model 240 D back in 1983. It was a 1981 model that they don't even make them anymore. It was now the year 2000 and I was still driving it. I did have some fun with a few other cars while I owned it, but the car that I hung onto was known as my sewing machine. That's what I named it because it was slow but reliable and I could count on it as I drove through the tapestry of life. Actually, I'd take slow and dependable any day, in love or cars.

So the day before my fiftieth, I bought my jeep. I drove to Tennessee to purchase it and made the journey back to North Carolina by way of the Smokey Mountains. What a way to break it in.

It turned out that the best present was yet to happen. I celebrated my fiftieth with my dad, who just turned 80. A special day. A true gift. I was "getting it." I was realizing what really matters in life. This book, Life Under Construction (LUC) talks about just that.

It is important to keep in mind the second part of my title, a Work In Progress. Life changes when we least expect it. The mountains remind me of this, especially when the trumpet daffodils persist in blooming bright yellow to signal the first sign of spring, only to be disguised under snow several days later. If we forget about the work part of life and start to coast too much, we just might be pleasantly surprised.

The soul should always stand ajar,
ready to welcome the ecstatic experience.

                      ❧ Emily Dickinson

Are You at Home in Your Life?

Home, sweet home. Sweet to look at, listen to, touch, smell and taste. The home is an emotional heartland, a place where the rhythm of events is under our control. The very word "home," derived from the Old Norse heima describes a state of being as well as a physical place.

Since I did not find the home I wanted to buy, I made the decision to build. It is a soul feeling of mine that we have a right and responsibility to construct our own life. And more importantly, if we don't, someone else will. That was sure true about building my home. If I did not take control, someone else would.

Just as it takes awhile for the ground to settle around a new house foundation, it takes time and space to settle after a life change. I keep hearing from people who are 50 years and older about these years being the best but I've only turned 50 in 2001 so the jury is still out as far as I'm concerned.

I have yet to settle down or settle in, as I write this, since my move. I do, however, feel confident that this is the place I am supposed to be, but it still is quite a change. I had been visiting North Carolina for about 20 years. The second I signed the contract to purchase my property, all .83 acres of it, I knew I was home. I'm at home in this country space where there is room to breathe.

You can feel at home anywhere "if you own" the space as yours and you really sense the special touches are yours alone. If it can't be an entire home, then make it a special room, or just a corner in a room. Create a place to think, to dig a little deeper, to create, or to just sit. Whether it's a room, a house, a state of mind, or corner space; it's mostly about being who you are at any given point in your life. We shape our homes. Thereafter, they shape us.

It's important to tune your home and life so that it restores the balance between mind and body. Home, Sweet Home. It's an emotional heart. Home can be described as a state of being as well as a physical place.

And now the big questions beg to be answered or at least it was that way for me.

Are you at home in your life?

Do you have clarity in your purpose on earth?

Are you living true to the values you profess to yourself?

Are you pretending to be someone else, or do you want what someone else has?

Is there anything you are hiding from?

What do you see when you look at your life?

What do you hear when you look inside and listen softly?

How are you spending your time?

OK! I asked a lot of questions, but this being at home in your life can be challenging.

Don't turn the page just yet. Read the above questions one more time. Now take a deep breath and just be still.

What happened?

PLANS

I peered at my computer for weeks, searching for the "right" plans for my home. The simple plan I had in mind might have been too simple. But I found what I could and improvised a little, and it seemed like it would work.

When I took the plans to the architectural review committee, they said they were too plain. Imagine that. OK, I said. I simply added a bit more design to the exterior, known as a dormer - which is another building, though small, that intersects the primary building along the roof's top. It passed this time. Luckily, an architect friend suggested several changes for the inside design to make it more functional, and it dramatically increased the usefulness of the space inside. His name is in the Acknowledgments if you need a talented and honest architect.

I found that if I stopped and asked myself the following questions when planning, I discovered more clarity:

What do I want my space to feel like?

Can I use all this space?

How important is light to me?

Do I have room to move around?

Does every space feel comfortable?

What do I want each room to feel like?

A floor plan should make the house feel comfortable and easy to live in.

What does your floor plan for life look like?

Year by year the complexities of this spinning world grow more bewildering and so each year all the more to seek peace or comfort in joyful simplicities.

First Floor 1/8"=1'-0"

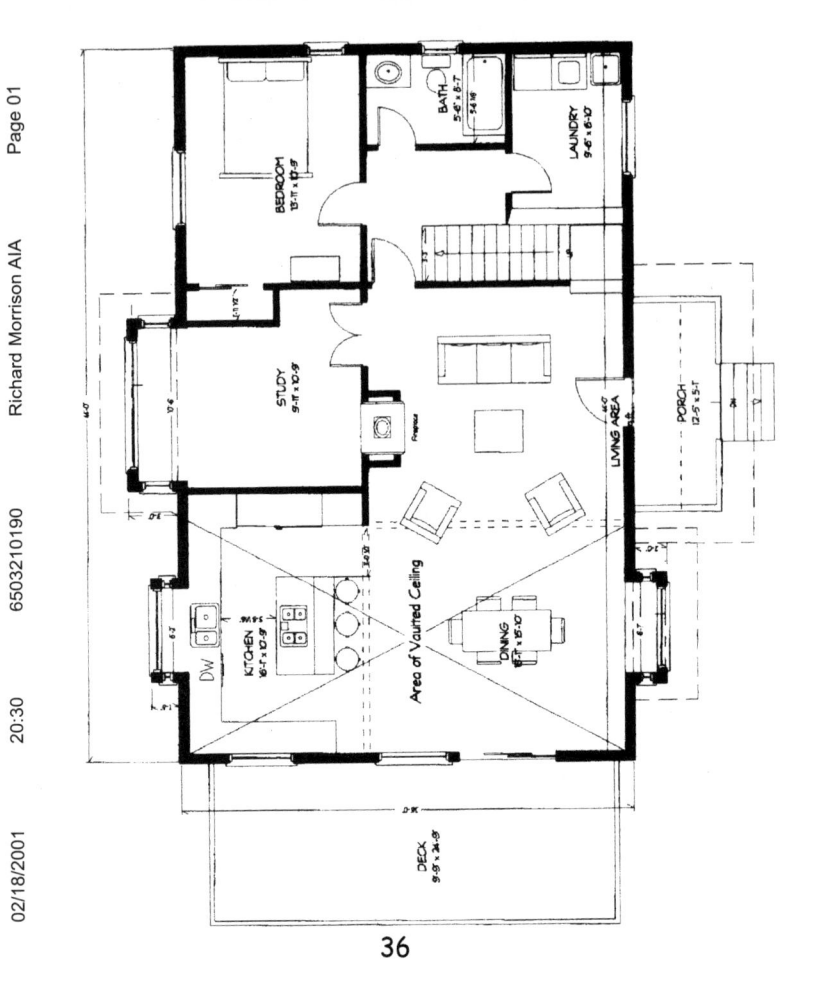

Richard Morrison AIA

02/18/2001   20:30   6503210190   Page 01

Second Floor 1/8"=1'-0"

02/18/2001   20:30   6503210190   Richard Morrison AIA   Page 02

Firing My GC

Sounds like a general contractor....Looks like a general contractor? Hmmm, I wonder.

Did you ever have a well-meaning friend or family member think that he or she could construct your life better than you?

It appeared that my dream "home" was becoming my general contractor's (GC) "house." His plan focused on a good product but always taking the path of least resistance, which in his situation meant saving money for him and me not getting what I wanted in my home. Understandable to some extent, but my dream mountain home was becoming his concept, not my vision. After many months of long distance communication over the phone (he did not have a computer or email, which should have been a clue), I finally made the journey back to North Carolina from California to meet him yet again, face to face. It was clear to me that our communication process was breaking down.

Finally, after he called me a name, which by the way was one of my favorite body parts, I made my decision to end that relationship. We didn't even get to exchange a handshake.

I did what any single, sane, 50-year-old woman would do when she had just moved across the country to live in the mountains of North Carolina by herself; I fired him. It translated to having no one to build my home. My decision was made to move, my house in California was sold and I was still moving, house or no house. I trusted my inner voice that was screaming to go ahead and build, even without a GC.

So, in essence, I started by stopping.

When I actually realized that I was in charge of building my own home, I had a rush of feelings. Fear visited every body part. Uncertainty and vulnerability ran rampant. Great excitement and anticipation on one hand and gaping holes of doubt sneaking in at the same time. Where to go from here?

I rushed the process. I tried one more time to find a general contractor. Okay, this time I'll try a woman. She lasted one month. When my house was supposed to be dried in, she did not even get her crew to put the felt on the roof in time for the heavy rain that at this time of the year was almost a daily occurrence.

Again, I revisited the thought, why not take over myself? Maybe this was another signal. I got in my car and rode the twisting curves to the town where the county office was, Sylva, and I pulled my own building permit, B1955. I decided I could do at least as well as they both did. I was capable. Not very knowledgeable but very determined.

I needed more copies of my plans but when I went to get them, it seems that my first builder was connected to the owner of the store where I was going to make copies of my plan. It is a small town. To my surprise and horror, they confiscated my plans. Not a good sign. Once again I felt a bit fearful and powerless.

Have you ever had plans that crumbled to rubble before your very eyes? Where to go next? That vague open space was scary and a bit stifling. I was frozen. I imagined myself in the middle of a Popsicle. Oh, you want to know the color. YELLOW!

And then I remembered. Life is always a work in progress. The best-laid plans need revising, reorganizing and rearranging. Once again, I started by stopping.

Do you need to stop for a minute?

The greatest gift

that you can give yourself

is a little bit of your own attention.

🌿 Anthony J. D'Angelo

Building Permit – The Smile before Reality Hit!

That's Rosie. She Owns the Diner Where Builders Gather for Food.
My Favorite Sign. No Cussing is Allowed.

CONFISCATED PLANS

Now it is one thing to have no plans at all, but to have someone confiscate your plans, well, that's another story. I want you to know that I had not breached any contract. Nothing had been signed. I had help with my plans from an architect friend and the general contractor had taken my plans and had them drawn up for me. Once again, I paid for them.

He decided that he was going to hold my plans hostage and somehow that would change my mind and I would be forced to continue with him. He arranged for this plan service store, which shall remain nameless - although I would love to tell the world - to take my copy of the plan and keep it. Now these were not cheap plans. Just to have a set copied costs about $35. Between the store and the builder, they had four sets of my plans. I was on a strict budget with the bank. If there ever was a time to doubt my decision to build by myself, this was really it. I guess he thought that he could push me into building with him. I have found that pushing someone into something usually doesn't work.

Luckily, I had one copy at home. So, I took my copy to have more copies made in another town close by. If I really believed in trusting the universe and my gut, now was the time to put up and shut up.

This is a hard lesson for me to get. It seems I must learn it over and over. I was questioning my decision to build. Did I have the ability to pull my own building permit and be the project manager for my own home? Did I have the stamina? Did I have the courage? Was I being foolish?

The worst part about not trusting is that when you worry, you drain your energy and creativity. You empty your mind and spirit from your soul. You lose direction and get fearful of life. Fear supports you staying at a standstill and you lose momentum, like stepping in gum on hot asphalt or getting stuck in second gear.

I read once in a book that at the bottom of every fear is simply the fear that you think you can't handle whatever life may bring you. You can diminish your fear by developing more trust in your ability to handle whatever comes your way. Taking a deep breath seems to help as well. Well, maybe two or three, depending on the situation. The better you feel about yourself, the more you can take on in life. Fear is natural when you are in unfamiliar territory and constructing your life. Expect it.

After all, it's just life in progress!

I've been absolutely terrified every moment of my life and I've never let it keep me from doing a single thing that I wanted to do.

&▲ Georgia O'Keeffe

LIFE BY DESIGN

Design it and get ready to change it. My simple drawing was actually too simple for the architectural review committee but with just one easy change, they accepted it. Life appears to me as a drawing. Always use a pencil, because you need to keep your eraser close at hand. Like food, an eraser can feed your soul, because it can give you an opportunity to erase what hurt in the past and let go of plans that are not working so that you can nurture the process. Knowing when to erase or let go of a sketch that you know is not working can be difficult. Sticky like honey that just won't let go of your finger, some plans are hard to drop.

We make ourselves up as we go along in life. Just like designing a house, we need to remember to design our life allowing enough flexibility for change. Keep your options open.

My goal when I moved to the mountains was to simplify my life.

So, my house design needed to be simple and yet have open spaces with lots of light.

I bought the book *The Not So Big House* by Sarah Susanka and it was full of practical advice. I have always been drawn to smaller, more personal spaces than larger, more expansive ones. I have lived in larger homes only to find that there were certain rooms I ignored completely, or I just did not feel comfortable when I spent time in those rooms. Maybe I'm not a formal kind of gal. Even when I eat breakfast, I'd rather sit at a small, cozy bistro table. I've always loved cafes.

I thought about the rooms in my last house that I enjoyed the most as I designed my new mountain home; lofts and nooks best describe the spaces I feel most creative around. Following is a list of the things I was not going to do without. After all, it was my fiftieth birthday present to myself. This may be my only chance. It was a post and beam home. There is wood galore, high ceilings and open spaces.

Here are some words and phrases that help identify the quality of space: cozy and introverted while inviting at the same time, light-filled yet casting interesting shadows, exciting and dramatic yet serene, sumptuous, homey and private and welcoming at the same time, impressive with a modest feeling, friendly with touches of elegance and delicate warmth, and inviting private edges with a common core. Often, houses today have ceilings that are the same height, leaving no way to differentiate between spaces. As you know by now, I need space to breathe, don't you? Timber frame spaces are "people friendly" and wonderfully comforting.

I hope the following information will help you to visualize the space I created.

A bay window. Big enough to sit and stare outside. I wanted to bring the outdoors indoors as much as I could. I remember sitting in my window once and watching a car drive by very slowly. Then it backed up. Then they pulled in my driveway, just to talk about my home. You guessed it; they were building a home of their own and wondered if they could see mine. I guess it was something about hanging out in my window that was inviting to them and I was fully clothed! Well, I wanted a window seat but I ordered a bay window, so I made a minor adjustment. You can't unring a bell!

A fireplace. I'll have two, thank you. I've always wanted a fireplace in my bedroom and now here was my chance. I'm also particularly proud of the living room fireplace because I did it myself. My hands will never forget the cold, rough, harsh touch of cement and stone. It's not very forgiving.

A Jacuzzi. Well, actually a Jacuzzi for two with windows over the tub so that I could open them and hear my stream. And a skylight to look up and watch the stars and moon.

Skylights. "Let there be light." I heard over and over when I was designing my home to watch out for the windows because they cost so much money. Well, windows let light into not only your home but also your life and penetrate into your soul. Windows help you to bring the beauty of nature into your home. I need light! Over and over, I heard, watch the skylights, because they leak, and once again, I listened to my heart's desire for light. Windows have a definite role in controlling the ambiance of a space.

I only put four skylights in and really wanted more, but one has to settle sometimes. One over my tub, as I just mentioned, one in the living room and kitchen, and one over my reading chair in the loft. I love to watch the skylight welcome the rain and the magical movement of the clouds drifting by and creating a dance.

A bookcase in the stairwell. Another one of my favorite places to read is on the stairwell. The stairwell is made of mountain laurel, a tree that curves and forms unusual shapes, found on my land. My bookcase forms an entire wall going up my stairs. It's fun to pick a step and a book and just read.

I don't want to bore you with too many details, but I hope the above will give you an idea of the space I live in. Of course, it is very cozy with a mountain feel.

Oh, one more thing. *No beige rooms.* My last home stayed beige the entire time I lived in it. Not this one. Pick a color. Barnyard red, moonmist, wildflower, candle glow, cashew, sequoia, olive fog, silver laurel, sage, and autumn acorn on the interior walls. The exterior color is chestnut brown and hunter green.

A home has a job and that job is to nurture and protect. Two weeks after I moved into my home, guests commented that it looked like I had been living there for years and years. Nesting had already taken place. My dream home is an expression of who I am. I knew this home was going to feel different. Partly because I had built it and knew it intimately before I even moved in. As a result of my role in building my home, every space in my home is used. It feeds my soul and awakens my spirit. It is comfortable and each room delights me. Just makes me want to shout, yahoo! And I do every morning.

Your home can do the same. Whether you design your home or a room in your home. Make it a special space. Let it speak to you.

Have nothing in your home that you do not know to be useful or believe to be beautiful.

🌿 William Morris

When we design our lives, we must be convinced that we are creative and that we have many talents. Really, I never thought, in my wildest dream that I would construct a stone fireplace.

A colleague of mine, Paula Statman, talks about creativity, and from her I learned to ask the questions below to help me tap into my creative self. Maybe they will help you.

Look behind you.

1) Have you lost something along the way?
2) What do people remember about you?

Look within yourself.

1) What strength do you use well?
2) Is there a strength that you are not using?
3) What would happen if you focused on just one strength?

Look to others.

1) What do people tell you about yourself? Ask for feedback.
2) Do you hang out with creative folks? You know, people that are doing what you would like to do?

My friend, Steve, builds houses for a living and he thought I could do it. I'm sure he had more confidence in me than I did, at least at the beginning.

Life needs to be designed as well. Mind, body and spirit all need our time and attention. Simple can be complicated because it takes more thought and planning.

The Fireplace I Built! Hard on the Hands.

Building a Home - a Different Animal

I'm often curious and amazed at myself that I believed I could build a home in the mountains. I mean, we are talking about paying attention to a budget that a bank is always reviewing and inspecting. Not being a numbers gal, I'm dyslexic and truthfully not very organized. I learned a few new skills fast.

I can remember an arrogant comment I made to give myself false confidence. It goes like this: Well, if I could get a doctorate in counselor education and psychology, I can build a house. I had determination enough to finish a marathon, so what's the problem? You've heard all the rumors, or should I say horror stories, about building a house. Well, most of them are probably true. This is an area where exaggerations are not necessary because the stories can be pretty hair raising.

Now I can proudly say that I have survived the Xenia, Ohio tornado, a Florida hurricane, a San Francisco earthquake and building a home in the mountains.

I was able to hone some skills in the process, such as making decisions and constantly working on a futuristic (meaning in the future I WILL be living in my home), creative and tolerant attitude and staying healthy.

Each day was a new lesson, with new words with weird meanings to learn. I stayed barely a breath ahead of my process some days. The amazing part to me, and probably my saving grace, was that the process could be measured every day, and progress was always forward. Even when it rained, I stopped by to clean up a bit and that felt good. I was over my head but kept right on treading and seemed to stay afloat.

There seemed to be a decision to make at least every hour, ranging from the very exciting kind such as plumbing pipes and heating and cooling systems, to how many outlets and where, what kind of windows, stone for the fireplace and others too numerous to mention.

And then there is an entire new language to learn. The choices never stop. Handling the budget, supervising a framing crew, and passing building inspections by the county were just part of everyday existence.

But a home in the mountains was what I wanted. And when you know you are living where you are meant to be, you just keep on keeping on!

The house is more than a box

within which to live;

it is a soul activity to be retrieved

from the numbness

of the world of modern objects.

🌱 Robert Sardello, *Facing the World with Soul*

Finally, A Place to Sit a Spell and Enjoy the View!

THE FIRST PEG

When I hammered the first peg of my post-and-beam home, I knew I was going to be able to build my home…one peg at a time.

Too often I think we just get stuck. We tend to fumble in one direction because we look at our lives and we experience it as if there is too much to handle; too many options, too many decisions, and too many obstacles. We don't stop long enough to obtain clarity.

As I mentioned earlier, I rushed the process because fear set in after I fired my first general contractor and did not carefully consider my second general contractor, who, of course, did not work out either. I took it as just another sign that I was to build my home myself.

At times we all seem to rush the process. We just plain get

ahead of ourselves. If, however, we take it one peg at a time, we make steady progress. Slow and steady.

A word about post-and-beam homes.

The first frame building appeared at about the time of the birth of Christ, according to Tedd Benson, author of *The Timber Frame Home*. For me, timbers draw the eye upward to the heavens and create a sense of balance and mystery. It reflects the forces of God and the universe. At the Great Buddha Hall in Japan, timbers were used both for structural and decorative purposes.

A timber frame that is made of wood, cracks, shrinks and twists. Buying quality sometimes means accepting the wrinkles, like the difference between man-made polyester, which can be made never to wrinkle, and the natural fiber of cotton, which has a certain comfort, feel, and texture. "Wrinkles" can also be seen as a drawback, but you know you have the real thing. The shrinking and checking of timbers is not to be taken lightly because it sounds a bit eerie, especially in the middle of the night! It is almost as if your home is talking to you. Many nights I have been suddenly awakened by the sounds of my home. You get used to it and almost welcome it because your home is continuing to live.

Well, it's time to build. Let's look at renovating, reconstructing and restoring.

How the eye loves a genuine thing;
how it delights in the nude beauty of the wood.

🍃 John Burroughs, naturalist

One Peg at a Time!

Exposed Ceiling Frames Provide a Sense of Rhythm.

Renovate your Mind

Repair, put into good condition.

Is your mind a dangerous neighborhood where you don't want to go alone?

Well, is it?

Yikes. That sounds a bit scary. But really, stop and think about it. The only thing we can control in this entire universe is our own minds. What we think. And as I learned from psychologist Dr. Albert Ellis, when I was working on my doctorate in psychology, what we think leads to how we feel, which leads to action. A simple concept, to be sure, but about as easy as getting the top off of a pill container that has a safety seal on it when your hands are slippery. Having said that, the concept is easy to remember but hard to put into practice.

Sometimes we give away our power and our mind control when we mistakenly assume that others can control how we think. Too often we tend to accept the words we hear from others as truth. Does this sound familiar? YOU make me feel so bad, mad, glad or sad. Accept your responsibility for your life. Don't give your power to live as you choose away to others. I can only remind you that other people, places and things do not control you in any way unless you let them. Situations happen and we control how we react to them.

Your circumstance don't make you, they reveal you!

ቈ Charles Swindoll

More important to note is that our attitude can make way for progress in constructing the life we want or in destructing that life. Being open and positive helps us to expand our minds and be more creative in our lives and thought processes. It also helps us to explore the creative part of our lives and gives us more confidence to take risks.

I wonder what is the first thing you think about when you wake up each day? Are you even aware of how you start each day? I choose to begin my day by reading the "Daily Word." Some of you are probably familiar with it. It is published by Unity School of Christianity. It simply gives you a word or two to focus on for that day. Today, as I write this, the word is "season of growth." It talks about relishing those times when your soul calls to be expanded.

When I was building my house, I would not be honest if I did not let you know that it was stressful. I am pretty good at handling stress, but I am thankful for the signals that my body gave me that indicated I needed to watch out when I was overdoing it. Maybe the warning sign wasn't strong enough, however, because I ignored it. It's in my history; what can I say? Anyway, in the morning I started noticing when I would brush my hair that I was losing more and more hair every day. Not a great way to start the day, and my thoughts were of a panic nature: "Great, I will have a beautiful home to live in but I won't have any hair." People will say something like, "great house, but what happened to your hair?" Probably a bit childish and extreme? Not a good way to start the day. So I took action. Because most of the work I was doing was around dust, my hair would be quite dirty at the end of the day. I decided to start washing my hair at night and brushing it so that when I woke up in the morning, I would at least have clean hair. Well, you might be laughing, but it worked. I just put it in a ponytail and put on my standard work outfit, overalls, and drove to the site.

<u>Your mind and creativity.</u> Statistics state that we are most creative at the ages of 2-4. So, I'm over 50, so you do the math! Our minds need to be in good thinking order if we are going to use our creative talents. They also have to be strong so that we can take some risks and get out on the edge. I worked hard on my creativity while I was building my home. Since I wasn't an "official general contractor" in the community, and still wanted to receive a 15% contractor's discount from the building supply store, I decided to try something. I went in with my most familiar tool. Not a hammer but my magic wand. Good news; it worked. Not only for that specific objective but also the entire store was talking about the event and they all got to know me, and fast. Of course, next time I wore my windshield-wiper glasses and then my wizard hat. Mixing a little fun with work.

Tool. Watch out for COPL! COPL stands for trying to Control Other People's Lives. Just work on your own thoughts. You'll get a lot further ahead and save lots of time.

*The only thing in the world you can change
is yourself
and that makes all the difference in the world.*

               ❧ Cher

Write down thoughts you need to give more attention to keeping or letting go!

_____

_____

_____

_____

Life is not a stress rehearsal.

               ❧ Loretta LaRoche

Reconstructing your time!

Reconstruct: to reframe, join together parts.

Are you making the future work for you by simplifying and prioritizing?

I am continually reconstructing the way I use my time, and one thing that I have discovered is that to simplify your life and time is hard work. I have something that happens in my mind at times. It is called the "terminally vague syndrome." My best attempt at describing this goes like this: My mind goes in too many directions at once. It is hard for me to remain focused. Other things that I am not working on seem more inviting than what I need to focus on. For example, writing this book. Even as I focus on writing, my mind goes to other related things and I get distracted. Yet, I know that disciplined focus gives me power and is really the only way I will succeed and complete this book.

*When you stay focused and keep a commitment
you create momentum,
and momentum creates momentum.*

≥● Rich Fettke

I love the word "focus" because in Italian, it means fireplace. A fireplace is the focus of light and heat and comfort. And that is what focusing brings me, the delight at making progress. Answering the following questions might give you an idea about your ability to focus.

1. Are you so creative that you produce multiple ideas, but they never get any action and follow-through?

2. When you are working on a project, does your mind tend to wander to other things? Often I work from my home office. When I take a restroom break, I might wander around my house getting

involved in other projects before I return to my office. Heck, this can delay me anywhere from 10 minutes to an hour. I believe it has to do with picking the path of least resistance.

3. Do you have clutter that you need to eliminate that creeps into your life and doesn't contribute to anything?

4. Do you have difficulty downsizing your daily activities?

Quit trying to cover all the bases at once. Stop responding to every opportunity and be selective. Narrow life to what is precious and necessary.

Think few and concentrate on the essentials. Avoid dissipated or splattered energy. Be intentional with your focus. How you spend your time is the only true measurement of what is important to you in your life.

> *You will always have time for the most important things but not if you do the unimportant things first.*
>
> 🌺 Stephen Covey.

Focus frees time rather than consuming a person. It can liberate. Instead of stretching us thinner, it can keep us from overextending ourselves.

Decide where your growth can make the biggest difference and then drive hard in that direction. Figure out what to ignore. That way you can cultivate, nurture and grow in that one or two areas.

TOOL. Let something drop. Yep, you heard me right. Drop it. What are you juggling in your life? I wanted to learn how to juggle. I realized that juggling balls was just too difficult for me. I needed more time. They were too heavy. I kept dropping one of them. One day, someone told me that I should try juggling scarfs. Why scarfs? They give me more time. I needed more time to be able to focus on the task at hand. And sure enough, I can juggle three scarves. Sometimes it takes more time to focus on what is important and to be brave enough to drop the ball on something that just doesn't cut it.

*When you focus on free time,
you multiply your productivity.*

🐌 Susan Corbett

What do you need to "let go" of?

_____
_____
_____
_____
_____
_____
_____
_____
_____

Let the future know what you want from it. The future cannot direct you if you don't know what you want. If you don't know where you are going, you will probably end up somewhere else.

Restoring your Energy

I have had jobs before where I worked about 90 hours a week, but building a home can be even more demanding than that. How was I to get through this? I would be on the job at sunrise, basically because I wanted to make sure I was paying only for the hours that people were on the job working. And I would usually be the last to leave, spending time cleaning up to get the site ready for the next day. The more I did, the less others had to do and the faster the process would flow. As I mentioned earlier, the house was built in about 7 months. Really good time for any home being built in the mountains, especially by an owner-builder.

Each day I would get home, I still had phone calls to make and a list to prioritize for the next day. Mind you, I am not complaining; I was tired but loving every minute of seeing my house being built. I was fortunate to be able to pull on the skills that got me through my doctorate program, and that would be determination to see things through to the finish and just enough of a compulsive personality to keep on keeping on.

It became clear that energy was one of my best resources as long as I followed some simple guidelines, which included making a list of priorities, not to exceed 10 on the list, and drop the rest. I needed to let go of things that I realized were not going to happen if I wanted to move into my home by fall. It was time to compromise and look at what I could live without. I had to let go of the items that were causing me undue anxiety, so I could free more energy. I had to caution myself not to just run on adrenaline!

And speaking of letting go of things to remember. Well, isn't that what "sticky notes" are made for? I used sticky notes in different colors, shapes, sizes and messages. Well, I still use them. Every morning, I would wake up with a special message or reminder on my computer.

Not only did I need to watch my energy but also keeping up my spirit during the process was a challenge. Mostly because I would vacillate between being so ecstatic when something went right and then discouraged when I blew it and my energy turned to low-level ecstasy.

TOOL. When you are learning a new skill, it is very important to be realistic about what you think you can achieve. I would be really encouraged at times and then greatly discouraged. Once again the lesson was in "letting go" of the things I could not control. At times when I did not know where to turn, I would just go outside and burn some leftover wood and clean up my site. Often that is a wise action to take in life as well.

I once read a book entitled Illuminata by Marianne Williamson. She states that part of our mind is bent on love, and part of it is bent on fear. We always have the choice to align ourselves with love and act accordingly or to give in to fear and, on some level die. The problem is that the voice of the spirit is not the dominant voice of the work; fear is louder than love.

I felt the negative ego and fear loudly and clearly. It was almost like an alarm going off in my head when I knew I was treading on unfamiliar territory, which was most of the time. I was faced with the belief that I had deep in my heart to trust the universe. And each day, I did just that. I managed to let my spirit shape my fear.

One of the greatest sources of energy

is pride in what you are doing.

❧ Voltaire

Lessons Learned

SIGNALS AND SIGNS IN THE UNIVERSE

When I was deciding if this California girl should turn country, several signs seemed to signal my direction. I had ordered a few knickknacks from a catalog for my house. What my order included, to my surprise, that I did not order, was a throw blanket with a picture of a log cabin and a bear. Now how would you interpret this? It wasn't even listed on the inventory-packing list, so I wasn't charged for it. Of course, I called and purchased it and now it is on the back of one of my living room chairs. It is the first thing I see when I walk through my front door. Just a reminder that I am where I am supposed to be.

I'm convinced there are many clues in the universe that are there to guide us, but often we are too busy to open our eyes or ears to receive them.

Are there signals in your life that you may be missing? You will, if you don't pay attention to them? Are you open to letting them in?

Trust yourself,

then you will know how to live.

   🌰 Johann Wolfgang von Goethe

Celebration of Country Living

A calmness brushes over me when I take time to admire the miracle of nature. Looking at the mountains tugs at my heart and helps me to keep life in perspective.

It took me awhile but to get real honest, I believe I landed here by grace. My need to be close to nature took over. My desire to live an authentic life seems to be easier for me after I slowed down. It is possible to slow down anywhere, I'm sure, but for me moving and living closer to old mountains seems to draw me in.

My walking buddy, Dori, who has lived here for a long, long time, reminds me of country ways, especially when she talks about my bear who "smooshed" my tree. Heck, I can't say it, much less spell it. But you get the idea.

Somehow we learn who we really are

and then live with that decision.

🌺 Eleanor Roosevelt

Mountain Moon

I awake and think surely it's morning because it is so bright outside but then realize it is too early for the sunrise. Ah, it's the full moon setting in the west shining in my window.

Positioning in life is a bit the same as positioning your house. I spent hours upon hours trying to get a fix on the right position for my house. What direction should it face? I wanted to see the sun rising in the morning and wanted the first opportunity to warm my house in the winter. I also wanted to view the sunsets to close out my day. And I am big on having as much natural light in my house as possible. I even considered the placement of the windows so that the moon would shine in my large picture windows on my second floor. I did not want to miss nature's light show. My house is set up so that I can follow the path of the sun from room to room.

Positioning myself in my career seems similar. There are

different ways to position. When I served as president of the board of directors for the National Speakers Association in Los Angeles, it was rarely about positioning for myself but more about positioning for relationships to work.

I am positioning my spiritual relationship with God. We talk a lot.

> *Only God knows our true needs.*
>
> ~ Mother Teresa

It seems in the mountains that you have a bit more time to think because the environment lends itself to just that. It can be so quiet and still that your mind opens to considering things about life that seem rather new and startling. My walks alone with the beauty and wonder of nature remind me to pause more frequently and consider the elements surrounding me.

What does positioning mean to you? Are you thinking about this for your future? What position is important for your relationships, your geographical location, your financial need and your spiritual connections?

Notes to myself: _____

_____

_____

_____

_____

_____

_____

_____

_____

_____

Bald Rock and Lake Fairfield.

My Three Mile Walking Trail Surrounds This Lake.

HANDLING IMPERFECTIONS

Get used to them! Even learn to welcome them.

When you are building your house or constructing your life, all lumber is not equal. There are imperfections wherever you turn. All builders are not equal. All subcontractors are not equal. You get the picture, I'm sure.

Work on permanence, not perfection. Work on progress, not perfection.

> *Perfection is self-abuse*
> *of the highest order.*
>
> ぁ Anne Wilson Schaef

Excuses are the nail used to build a house of failure.

🌺 Don Wilder *(contributed by my Dad)*

I've Got an Itch.

Oh, I'm probably painting a colorful masterpiece about my life in North Carolina. Better mix a few realities that annoy me so that you don't think I'm too blissful.

1. Chiggers. They like me and bite me. My entire legs were covered once with chigger bites when I was building my home. I got tired and sat down in the wrong place.

2. Getting behind a tractor forces me to slow down. Not a bad thing, actually.

3. No DSL. Enough said. Although, I believe, there is a way to speed things up with a cable connection.

4. K-mart and Wal-Mart are 30 minutes away. And those are the good places to shop. Actually, this is okay as well because the trip gets me off the mountain.

5. My wardrobe has changed drastically. It consists of fleece, fleece and more fleece in the winter. The rest of the year, it is jeans, jeans and more jeans.

Gosh, I guess I did not come up with a very convincing list.

*We either make ourselves miserable,
or we make ourselves strong.
The amount of work is the same.*

ة‌ Carlos Castaneda

Mental Preparation

Trusting yourself to know in your gut that you are doing the right thing is never an easy experience. Helen Keller said, "Life is either a daring adventure or nothing at all." Even small things can be daring. Anytime we move outside of our comfort zone, it is a risk.

I moved to North Carolina on March 27th, 2001. I've survived all four seasons, twice! The second winter was a bit rougher for me. I vow to get to a warmer climate in January and February from now on.

I am still working on this book as the summer of 2003 draws to a close. While there is still a small corner of my mind that wonders why it took me so long to finish my book, the time has afforded me a more accurate view as I look back at the life I have constructed. This November, I will have lived in my home for two years. Well, I guess it is time to sell and start constructing again.

Just kidding. Well, maybe not?

I'm clear on two things:

1. The mountains are very soulful to me. Yesterday I woke up and looked outside my bedroom window, and to my delight I witnessed seven turkeys in my driveway. Seeing nature so close reminds me to take note of creatures that share the earth with us. Nature offers us so many lessons if we just stay still long enough to learn them.

2. Right now I don't want to travel much. Although it may be necessary in the future, I feel it's important to make the effort to work more locally. In addition to marketing hard to speak locally, I just finished my real-estate course and passed my test. I am officially a North Carolina licensed real estate-salesperson. A move toward my goal to stay at home more. My mental preparation involved knowing I would love where I would be

living, but I still needed to earn enough to live there. So far, I am making it. Not sure if I will like it, but I'm going to give it a whirl.

Yes, I'll find you a perfect lot or home in Cashiers. Since I love living in this mountain space, it will be easy for me to show others what this land has to offer.

It seems that changes come in chunks!

The best place to find a helping hand is at the end of your arm.

ઢ Swedish proverb

What do you need to prepare your mind for?

So, This is What Snow Looks Like.

THE ONE UNKNOWN

A friend and I have a saying when things seem to get vague and directionless. For times when we seem to have no control over our situations, which is always. It goes like this: there is only "one unknown." This is always followed by laughter. Somehow it eases the fact that things are spinning in a direction that seems to be out of control. We both really know that everything is virtually unknown. We think we know what is ahead for us in our life. Who are we really trying to fool?

It is the same when you look at living the life you want. Let it flow.

Moonshine to Champagne

Before moving into my mountain home, I knew how to sip champagne and now, thanks to my CAT operator, I know how to survive a gulp of moonshine.

George cleared my land for my home site and put in my septic system. He truly is a mountain man. In fact, his appearance might even startle you at first glance, especially in the daylight. He was recommended to me by a friend who warned me, so I was not taken aback. George was awesomely unlovely.

One late afternoon I was running out of steam and it hit me. George brings a thermos every day and I was pretty sure he would share some coffee with me. I must have stared endlessly at it, like one looking up at the sky on a starry, starry night because he finally offered me a drink from his thermos. I asked him if he would mind if I just had a small cup of coffee. He smiled with all four of the teeth he had left and said, "Honey, that ain't coffee; it's moonshine." I thought that one swig couldn't hurt too much and it was too late to turn back now without offending him, so I took a sip. My skin was tingling all the way down to my toes. After I caught my breath and my eyes stopped bulging, I smiled. Our friendship began.

I gained more confidence in my role of general contractor because if I could communicate with him, I just might be able to tackle all of my subcontractors.

When you are tackling a huge project, it's important to celebrate every success, no matter how small.

What started out as moonshine ended up with a celebration of champagne in my new home.

What do you have to celebrate?

Friendships multiply joys

and divide griefs.

🍃 H.G. Bohn

P.S. Drink champagne, not moonshine.

Moving In

Seven months, 6 hours and 22 minutes later, I moved into my home just in time for Thanksgiving. Perfect timing, because I was so thankful that the project was finished and I had a place to call home.

I even had an unexpected Thanksgiving dinner guest, even though I'm not a good cook. But the bear on my deck didn't know that. I wondered what I had gotten myself into as I crouched behind my bar in the kitchen trying to gain confidence and courage from a friend on the phone. He had previous experience with bears. Finally, after 5 minutes of whimpering, shaking and my heart beating too fast to even count the beats, I mustered enough courage to grab my camera and take the photo from an inside window.

When I moved in, I already had a sense of knowing the space as if I had already lived there. My connection was very personal.

knew every nook and cranny intimately. After all, I was living with it in my head for a long time and had visited every room, corner and deck. This time I could stay the evening as well as all day. I did not have to leave. Tomorrow I would open my eyes and the picture in my head of sleeping in my own bed in my new home would be a reality.

I thought I would sleep like a well-fed baby after burping but my excitement kept me awake most of the night. I had built my dream house. I pulled the permit, passed the inspections. I made sure all the parts were moving. It started by clearing the property and rearranging some dirt on a wonderful piece of land with a view and a stream. I was occupying the space I helped create and calling it home.

Compose materials as a melody. Notice those that support and underscore and those that offer counterpoint. Keep the progression slow and notice the view. Allow the house to dance.

My Thanksgiving Day Guest.

WRITE YOU OWN BUILDING PERMIT

We make ourselves up as we go along.

It's kind of like writing your own building permit. Oh, we pretend and "act as if" we have control but most of the time most of us fake it. We make informed decisions but really forget that we control very little of what can actually happen. The more we try to control, the more we use up valuable resources, such as time and energy.

My goal when I moved to the mountains was to simplify my life. I am confident I have used quality building materials. My plan and design have become a reality. A living and breathing structure.

What does your building permit look like now? Are you satisfied with the plans you have drawn? Have you taken time to question and appraise the design? If you could write your own permit, and you can, what would it look like? Care to draft it now?

_____
_____
_____
_____
_____
_____
_____
_____
_____
_____

Here are two of my favorite quotes by an accomplished and talented builder. You might know her by now. Her name? Maryellen Lipinski, of course.

You can never live anyone else's life.

🕯 Mel

*Design your own building permit
and then you will be home.*

🕯 Mel

Why not pick up your tools and start building your future now?

*No one succeeds beyond their wildest
expectations unless he or she begins with some
wild expectations.*

🕯 Ralph Charey

END

So much has changed since I started writing this book, as it always does in life. Yes! The best-laid plans often need reconstructing, reframing, remodeling and restoring. I love the mountains even more than I thought possible and walking around the three-mile lake does my heart good.

One of my best friends and a major reason that motivated my move to the mountains turned out to be a connection that doesn't seem to be lasting. It feels like what Bill Bryson wrote in his book A Walk in the Woods: "There was an odor between us. An unhappy sense that things had changed and would not be the same again." I felt it. Stranger yet, she never understood it. We would never get too close again. This revelation is not meant to be mean and hurtful. It was, however, a harsh reality that came with my move to the mountains. But hey, it was another reminder that we just keep constructing and building the life that lies ahead of us.

Wouldn't it be nice to secretly have someone run along side of you in life and be your best friend, just like a trusting dog does?

> *To offer no resistance to life is to be in a state of grace, ease, and lightness.*
> *This state is then no longer dependent upon things being in a certain way, good or bad.*
>
> 🐾 Eckhart Tolle, *The Power of Now.*

Sometimes we get wake-up calls in life. I can still remember taking a long, slow, deep breath and the relief I felt when I decided to move to the mountains. Much like being somewhere when you had to go to the restroom really bad but there wasn't any in sight. And finally, comfort. Or how your nerves feel after a close call, when you saw a car coming toward you and thought it was going to hit you.

Building my home gave me a certain degree of increased self-confidence about tackling future life projects and adventures. Maybe even a bit more courage. Before I built my home, I would have laughed at myself for even entertaining thoughts about my next move. It would have just been a dream in my head. But now, I believe I can make my next dream, not just in living Italian color in my mind, but a reality. Unfulfilled desires are dangerous choices.

My home, named Belvedere ("beautiful view" in Italian), and also one of my favorite Polish vodkas, is a place that gives space to my spirit. It makes my heart beat faster. It is the corner of my life. It is my emotional space to restore my balance.

And life goes on, as life always does. It is a work in progress. And always will be.

Stuff to fix and repair, hammers and sanders to help fine-tune, and screwdrivers to tighten loose parts...just like life. There will always be a bit of reframing. *Just a work in progress.*

Restoration and renovation are still necessary. Sound familiar? Some assembly still required. Just like life.

*Dreams and dedication
are a powerful combination.*

❧ William Longgood *(contributed by my Dad)*

Why can't life be smooth and seamless? It just isn't.

I became the architect of my future.

I designed the life I wanted to live.

What a feeling to be at home in my life. La Dolce Vita - the sweet life.

As I sit on my back deck, my eyes wander over the mountain ridge and I begin quietly turning up the volume to listen to yet another dream in my head. As I take note of the sun rising, I entertain another adventure and envision a farmhouse in Tuscany, in a small Italian Village...but that's another story, or should I say, my next book.

Ciao,   *Maryellen*

We must be ready to get rid

of the life we've planned,

so as to have the life

that is waiting for us.

🐌 Joseph Campbell

ORDER FORM

Ship to:
Name:_____

Address:_____

City:_____State:_____Zip:_____

Additional copies of Life Under Construction:
By Maryellen Lipinski, Ed.D.

Quantity: _____

Total for books ($12.95 each) _____

Shipping
($3.50 first copy, $2 additional copy) _____

Sales Tax (NC 7%) _____

Also available:

Random Thoughts and Mine Always Are………

Conscious Detours to Creative Power! @ $12.95 _____

TOTAL: _____

Ordering information on the back of this form.

Send your order to:

Maryellen Lipinski
LUC Press
142 Eagle Ridge Rd. #2015
Sapphire, NC 28774

Phone: 828-743-9600
Fax: 828-743-9817
Email: maryellen@maryellenlipinski.com
www.maryellenlipinski.com